Untitled Poems

Sujata Gautam

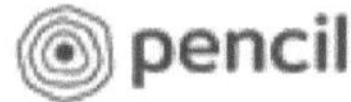

ISBN 978-93-5610-990-2
© Sujata Gautam 2022
Published in India 2022 by Pencil

A brand of
One Point Six Technologies Pvt. Ltd.
123, Building J2, Shram Seva Premises,
Wadala Truck Terminal, Wadala (E)
Mumbai 400037, Maharashtra, INDIA
E connect@thepencilapp.com
W www.thepencilapp.com

All rights reserved worldwide

No part of this publication may be reproduced, stored in or introduced into a retrieval system, or transmitted, in any form, or by any means (electronic, mechanical, photocopying, recording or otherwise), without the prior written permission of the Publisher. Any person who commits an unauthorized act in relation to this publication can be liable to criminal prosecution and civil claims for damages.

DISCLAIMER: *The opinions expressed in this book are those of the authors and do not purport to reflect the views of the Publisher.*

Author biography

Sujata Gautam is a writer, whose most of her work is inspired by real-life situations, experiences, and observations. She likes to do painting, cook, read, and write. A young girl with big dreams in her little eyes. Passionate about giving and contributing something better to this world. She believes in expressing her emotions without hesitation and living life without worrying about the future and results. She participated in various cultural activities and competitions during her school life, in her school, city, and district, which taught her to enjoy unpredictable life and not to miss any opportunities standing before her. Slowly and steadily she learned the lesson that, 'This is life and it is meant to be lived, not to win.'

CONTENTS

Untitled 1 9

Untitled 2 10

Untitled 3 11

Untitled 4 12

Untitled 5 14

Untitled 6 15

Untitled 7 16

Untitled 8 17

Untitled 9 19

Untitled 10 20

Untitled 11 21

Untitled 12 22

Untitled 13 23

Untitled 14 24

Untitled 15 25

Untitled 16 26

Untitled 17 28

Untitled 18 29

Untitled 19 30

Untitled 20 32

Untitled 21 33

Untitled 22 34

Untitled 23 35

Epigraph

This is life and it is meant to be lived, not to win.

Preface

"Untitled Poems" is a collection of poetries by "Sujata Gautam". When the author participated in various anthologies, there she was asked to give a title to her poem, she remembered that her work has no title, while writing poems, she just penned down on paper whatever she felt, observed, experienced, or imagined but never gave a title to it. But now as she is participating in an anthology so it was necessary to give a title to her work. She started thinking about what title should she provide to it, so she picked some words from her poem and gave a title to it. Then whenever she participated in any anthology this struggle continued, she always found it difficult to give a title to her work, she tried different ways of doing this but was never satisfied with whatever title she give. And that was the time when the concept of this book was generated in her mind. She started asking herself why is it so necessary to give a title or name to any work? If my work looks better without any name or title, then why it could not remain like that? If it looks more amazing, suitable, and beautiful, without a title then why can't let it remain like that. Will it be not considered as amazing as it is without the title? And then she decided to launch her poetry collection, with the title "Untitled Poems" because she believes that art or work is beautiful without a title or name also, as it is the result of feelings, emotions, observations, or experiences of the artist, author or creator.

Untitled 1

Some steps far from here,
There's countryside,
Beneath the sky,
Filled with bright light.
Let's go there,
Will sit with a butterfly,
See some bird's beautiful flights,
And will let our body get energized in the sunlight.
There freedom and peace are felt at a time.
Come let's go there,
Just for a while.

Untitled 2

Whenever your mind feels disturbed,
When your heart craves some peace,
And when life seems vague
Listen to your old favorite songs
Escape reality for some time,
Close your eyes for a while,
And let your brain feel relieved.

Untitled 3

The bodies of loved ones are still not found,
we don't know if they are burned in the fire,
flown in a river,
or buried underground.
The pages of history narrate aloud,
this was a time when several servants of justice were found at fault.
It's been three decades passed when that terrible scene happened.
Memories of which still terrify their heart,
like being hit by a weapon.
Eyes are still in wait,
seeking justice and their rights.
Breeds are still asking the question and trying to trace,
"What was their fault on that day in that riot"?

Untitled 4

You are a blessing sweetheart.

Your smile,

The way you walk,

the way you talk,

Is so amazing.

The way you hesitate,

the way you bend your head down.

All are so amazing.

The way you listen to me so carefully,

the way you look at me,

the way you say hii from far with that beautiful smile and shyness on your face,

Everything is so amazing.

The way you so say sorry after every fight with those tiny tears in your big eyes,

The way you hug me,

the way you rub my hand to give me warmth in those cold mornings,

The way you come with me to drop me and then look and wait till I don't fade away in distance.

Everything is so amazing sweetheart.

The way you respect everyone,
the way you care about everyone,
The way you take all your responsibilities,
The way you try your best,
The way you don't harm anyone,
Is so amazing,
Your soul is so amazing sweetheart,
The way we feel about each other,
The way we understand each other,
The way we praise each other,
The way we accept flaws of each other,
All are so amazing.
Together we are so amazing sweetheart.

Untitled 5

Just guess who made me smile like this?

It's you and your love.

Just guess what made me so beautiful like this?

It's your care and support.

Just guess what made me so hardworking and dedicated to my work,

It's you standing far from me, near my goal.

It's the hope of reducing the distance between us by reaching my goal.

Just guess why I came closer to myself?

It's you residing inside me.

Just guess when I learned to see things deeply?

It's the moment when I learned that from you.

Just guess what made me strong like this?

It's our bonding.

Just guess what made me smile like this?

It's you as my inspiration.

Untitled 6

I got addicted to your fragrance so much,
that tried to find it in every perfume shop of the city,
but when came home defeated,
realized that it was already in my clothes,
making me tipsy day and night.

Untitled 7

Happiness is like sunlight,
it is going to come to you anyway,
but if you will open yourself it will come in more amount,
like the light through the window.

Untitled 8

A girl mad in love,
Mad for love,
And mad about love,
Let her in her world only.
She's not married nor is in a relationship,
She's just in love,
And let her be there only.
She's not someone's wife
nor anybody's girlfriend,
She is somebody's inspiration,
And let her be that only.
She wants respect also,
Not new dresses, jewelry, and accessories only.
She's also having her mind to take decisions,
Not made to follow others only.
Her thoughts are also beautiful,
Not body only.

She's not daddy's princess or husband's queen.

She's her goddess

And let her be that only.

Untitled 9

I can't tell you how much I love you,
thus I'm telling this to the universe,
Maybe it would tell you.

Untitled 10

Nothing can be more beautiful than saying and listening to the word, "Mummy".

Nothing can be more beautiful than making love to your child and getting loved by your mom.

Nothing can be more beautiful than dressing up your child and being dressed up by your mom.

Nothing can be more beautiful than keeping your child's head on your heart and keeping your head on your mother's heart.

Nothing can be more beautiful than giving birth to your child and getting birth from your mom.

And Nothing can be more beautiful than becoming a mother and getting raised by your mom.

Untitled 11

Life is not a joke,

Then why are you taking it so lightly?

Life is not a game,

Then why are you playing with it?

Life is too short,

Why are you not realizing that?

Time is passing like sand slipping through the fist.

So are you waiting for emptiness?

Or for the end?

Life is not the loud laugh of a joke,

It is not yell

It's the beautiful smile came to your face after seeing your loved one,

It's a drop of tears that came from eye on meeting someone after a long time.

It's that peace of your heart that you feel after getting a glance of your loved one with whom you were resent.

Untitled 12

Mujhe yun lat lagi hai tumhari khusbu ki,

Ki ab talab lagi hai apni sanson mein tumhe bharne ki,

Hamesha salah di thi maine tumhein vyasan mukt hone ki,

Par aaj tumhe mehsoos karne ki chah mein, Khwaahish huyi hai ek sigrette jalane ki.

Vo saansein jinhein nafrat thi uss dhuye se,

Aaj lalsa huyi hai unhein usey mastishk tak utar kar,

Dil ko kuch rahat pahunchane ki,

Mujhe yun lat lagi hai tumhari khusbu ki,

Ki ab talab lagi hai apni sanson mein tumhe bharne ki.

Untitled 13

And someday all this pain will be proven worthy,
And someday all your scars would be admired,
And someday your brown complexion would be desired.
The qualities which are known weak today
Would be proved strong someday
Tears falling from your eyes will melt people's heart someday,
And someday your head will feel light.
And someday your stained character is going to feel bright.

Untitled 14

Aaj maine ek ladke ko dekha,
Wo thoda thoda tumhare jaisa dikhta hai,
Usko muskurate dekha to tumhari muskan yaad aa gayi,
Usi ke sath aankhon mein thodi nami bhi aa gayi,
Par vo jab kareeb aaya
to yaad aaya ki,
Yeh tum nahin ho.
Yahan dhup fir khili hai,
Par ab tum nahin ho.
Haan vo kuch kuch tumhare jaisa jarur dikhta hai,
Par mere sath pura nahin jachta hai.
Yun baar baar mere veham ka tut jana,
Mujhe yaad dilata hai,
Yahan zindagi mein do pal ka pyaar to hai,
Magar phir unmr bhar ka intezaar hai.

Untitled 15

Maine kuch dil ki baatein kahin thi,
Jo tumhe nahin sunni chahiye.
Kuch prem patr likhe the,
Jo tumhe padhne nahin chahiye.
Kuch jazbaat zahir kiye the,
Jo tumhe nahin janne chahiye.

Untitled 16

Zara gor se suno iss raat ke sannate ko,

Yeh un striyon ke sath huye duskarm ka saalon se sok mana raha hai,

Yeh un gareeb kisanon ki majburi aur bebasi ke aansun baha raha hai.

Yeh vo kahani bata raha hai jisko suna nahin gaya,

Kuch to ankaha sa hai jo yeh suna raha hai.

Isne to kayi akal mrityun ke dard ko khudmein samaya hai.

Dekho kitna daravna hai na yeh,

Haan mujhe bhi dar to bohot lag raha hai.

Magar yeh mann maan hi nahin raha hai,

Aaj Innke dard ko sunke hi jana hai,

Isi zidd pe ada hai.

Aur inn zadiyon ko hata ke yahan poonam ke chand ki roshni ko lana hai.

Yahi guhar baar baar laga raha hai.

Zara gor se dekho iss raat ke andhere ko,

Dekho kaise ashq baha raha hai.

Yeh ashq jo inn patto pe aa gire hain,

Umeed hai nayi kiran ke sath yeh lupat ho jayenge.

Aur yeh patte subah roshni se fir khilkhilayenge.
Zara gor se suno iss raat ke sannate ko,
Shayad yeh saalon se nyay ki mang kar raha hai.

Untitled 17

Maana ki main apni baat sabko batati hun,
Par dukh jo sirf tumhein sunati hun,
Fir kyun tumhe aisa lagta hai ki,
Tumhein main khaas nahin manti hun.
Maana mehfil mein sath hote hain sath sabhi mere,
Magar tumhare kandhon pe fisalte hain ashq,
Aankhon se bahein jo kabhi mere.
Pata nahin na janein fir bhi kyun tumhein aisa lagta hai ki,
Tumhein main apna nahin manti hun.
Maana ki, theharne vale sabhi musafiron ko main apne paas bithati hun,
Par mayus ghadi mein jo sirf tumhein gale lagati hun,
Fir kyun tumhein aisa lagta hai ki,
Tumhein main paraya manti hun.

Untitled 18

Kuch chizein bikhri huyi hain to unhein bikhra hi rehne do,

Wo bikhri huyi hi zyada achi lagti hain.

Aur kya kaha aapne, ki maine aapka dil todd diya.

Arey koi baat nahin meri jaan kuch chizein tutne ke baad zyada khubsurat lagti hain.

Aur aap janna chahte ho na ki kyun main hanmesha aapke sath nahin reh sakti,

Kyunki dharti aasman se dur hi achi lagti hai.

Apni apni manzil ko jaa rahe the hum,

Itefaq se kuch dur ke liye hamare raste ek hi the,

Raste ekbar ko hamare ek ho sakte hain

Magar manzilein to sabki alag hi hoti hain na.

Chalo maan liya ki aapki jaan hun main,

Lekin jaan ko bhi to ekdin ye deh tyag ke apne ghar jaana hain na.

Chalo ab khushi khushi mujhe vida karo,

Phool ko bagh se juda hokar mehfil ko bhi to sajana aur mehkana hain na.

Untitled 19

Uska kajal thoda bikhra tha,
Aansuon se nahin pasine ke sath palkon se fisla tha.
Aanchal thoda maila tha,
Navjaat ke aansuon se bheega tha.
Baal uljhe huye the,
Bilkul uski tarah pyaar se bandhe nahin,
Jabardasti kisi se fanse huye the.
Aankhein thaki thi,
Chakachond se pareshan,
Niche jhuki thi.
Juban pe koi shikayat nahin thi,
Honthon ki laali bhi aadhi chut chuki thi,
Bilkul usi ke sarir ki tarah sukh gayi thi aur fiki pad chuki thi.
Kadam manzil ki taraf badh rahe the,
Mano payal se chalte rehna seekh rahe the.
Mausam usey satata tha,
Chanv usey bulati thi,
Aur uski bindi mujhe batati thi,

Vo koi kamzor ya bechari nahin,
Balki sahas se saji ek naari thi.

Untitled 20

Aankhein meri dhundh rahi hain kisiko,

Na jane kiski talash hai inko,

Pata nahin kiska intezaar hai inko,

Jane kyun yeh hanmesha takti hain sadkon ko?

Barson se jiski raah dekhi,

Kyun Radha ko hanmesha lagta hai ki,

Vo Krishna aane wala hai ab to?

Untitled 21

Yeh mere ashkon ki dhara thamti nahin hai,

Dukh mein chalakti hai, Khushi mein fisalti hai,

Juda hone par behti hai,

Gale lagne par bhi kahan rukti hai,

Vaise bhi to dil ki zamin sukhi padi hai,

Ab jo kuch baaki bachi namin hai,

Lagta hai ab yeh bhi aankhon se beh jayegi,

Aur ye dharti banjar ho jayegi.

Aur uss par ye dasht ki dhup jaise tez logon ka sitam,

Shayad banzar dharti ko bhi andar tak tod jayega.

Fir kahan kabhi kisi ko yeh yakeen aayega,

Ki yeh dhara bhi kabhi behad mulayaam thi aur beshumar mehakti thi.

Iske jehan mein bhi koi aasha palti aur panapti thi.

Kyun ab wo aisi ho gayi hai,

Kya baarish ki bundein usse runth gayi hain,

Ya fir ab uski unmar hi khatam ho gayi hai.

Untitled 22

Acha suno na,

Maine suna hai ki ishq mein zindagi badi khubsurat lagne lagti hai,

To phir chalo ek dafa iss zindagi se hi ishq karke dekhte hain.

Aur phir khushi ke aayine mein apne chehre ka noor dekhte hain.

Waqt thoda sab kaamon se chura ke kabhi khud se milne chalte hain.

Chor ke fikr aur zikr duniya ka,

Aao apni baat rakhte hain.

Shorgul ke iss jahaan mein,

Kahin kisi kone mein sukoon ke do pal dhudhte hain.

Kaafi thak chuke iss safar mein,

Chalo ab ghar chalte hain.

Untitled 23

Ghuma phira kar ek baat kehni hai,

Sirf uss ko samajh aaye aisi koi chitthi likhni hai,

Mujhe maalum hai zubaan keh nahin payegi,

par aankhon ne tumhari,

mere dil tak tumhare dil ki baat bheji hai.

Sirf tumhein mehsoos ho aisi tohfe mein maine tumhein kuch sogaat bheji hai,

Jante ho woh kya hai,

Mere honthon se pahunchkar tumhare honthon pe aa jaye,

Maine tumhein apni ek muskaan bheji hai.

~ a girl mad in love.

Printed by Libri Plureos GmbH in Hamburg, Germany